D1716337

Dirty Jobs
Farmhand

Kaite Goldsworthy

MEDIA ENHANCED BOOKS
AV2 BY WEIGL™
ADDED VALUE • AUDIO VISUAL

www.av2books.com

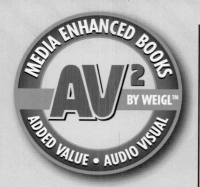

AV² provides enriched content that supplements and complements this book. Weigl's AV² books strive to create inspired learning and engage young minds in a total learning experience.

Your AV² Media Enhanced books come alive with...

Audio
Listen to sections of the book read aloud.

Key Words
Study vocabulary, and complete a matching word activity.

Video
Watch informative video clips.

Quizzes
Test your knowledge.

Embedded Weblinks
Gain additional information for research.

Slide Show
View images and captions, and prepare a presentation.

Try This!
Complete activities and hands-on experiments.

... and much, much more!

Go to **www.av2books.com**, and enter this book's unique code.

BOOK CODE

Q 6 4 1 4 7 1

AV² by Weigl brings you media enhanced books that support active learning.

Published by AV² by Weigl
350 5th Avenue, 59th Floor
New York, NY 10118
Websites: www.av2books.com   www.weigl.com

Library of Congress Control Number: 2014934870

ISBN: 978-1-4896-0994-6 (hardcover)
ISBN: 978-1-4896-0995-3 (softcover)
ISBN: 978-1-4896-0996-0 (single user e-book)
ISBN: 978-1-4896-0997-7 (multi user ebook)

Printed in the United States of America in North Mankato, Minnesota
1 2 3 4 5 6 7 8 9 0   18 17 16 15 14

032014
WEP150314

Project Coordinator: Aaron Carr
Designer: Mandy Christiansen

Every reasonable effort has been made to trace ownership and to obtain permission to reprint copyright material. The publishers would be pleased to have any errors or omissions brought to their attention so that they may be corrected in subsequent printings.

Weigl acknowledges Getty Images as its primary image supplier for this title.

Contents

What Is a Farmhand?

A farmhand is a person who works on a farm. Farmhands help with the daily running and managing of the farm. They perform many different jobs, depending on the type of farm they work on. They may care for animals, work with plants, maintain and operate machinery, build and repair farm buildings, or carry out any number of other jobs the farmer needs done.

There are about 2.2 million farms in the United States. Farming, or agriculture, is a very important job. It provides food as well as raw materials used to make other products such as clothes.

Many Names, One Job

Farmhands are known by many different names. The name often depends on the type of farm they work on or which country they work in. A ranch hand works on a ranch, helping to care for and move herds of **livestock**, such as cattle. In Australia, men and women who work with cattle or sheep as farmhands are called jackaroos and jillaroos.

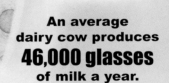

An average
dairy cow produces
46,000 glasses
of milk a year.

**World's Largest
Corn Producer**
the United States has
84 million acres
(33,993,594 hectares)
of corn.

Most of the farms in the United States are owned and operated by individuals or family companies.

Where They Work

Farmhands work on many different kinds of farms. Farms are usually located in rural areas, out in the countryside. Farmhands often spend much of the day working outside. They work year-round in all kinds of weather.

Sunrise to Sunset

Farmhands can work long hours, starting their day when the Sun rises. Seasonal work such as **harvest** time, fruit or vegetable picking, or when animals give birth to their young can mean even longer days.

Farmhands often work longer hours during harvest. Many farmers hire extra farmhands during this busy time of year.

During calving or lambing season, farmers and farmhands may need to get up to check on animals during the night. They have to make sure the mothers and new babies are doing well. Some of a farmhand's jobs are completed daily. Farmhands must feed livestock, put them out to **graze**, and clean their pens and stalls every day, including weekends. Dairy farmhands may help milk cows up to three times each day.

Working as a farmhand can be a very physical job. A small, square bale of hay can weigh up to 70 pounds (31.5 kilograms).

A Dirty Job

Most days, farmhands work outside with animals or in dusty or muddy places. Cleaning, or "mucking out," livestock stalls is a very dirty, smelly job. Farmhands must clean out the **manure** that the animals leave behind. The farmhands move the waste to another area of the farm, away from the animals and people. They also replace old hay and straw. If a farm has many animals, farmhands may need to muck out the stalls throughout the day.

Dangers on the Farm

Farms can be very dangerous places to work. Nearly 120,000 people are injured on farms in the United States each year. Livestock on the farm could bite or kick. Farmhands must be careful not to startle the animals and approach quietly, allowing the animals to see and hear them. Hand-washing is very important when working with livestock. Germs, bacteria, and infections can spread to humans and other animals.

Farmhands must be extra careful when working with large, heavy animals such as cows and horses. Injuries can happen accidentally.

Farms use poisonous chemicals, such as **pesticides** and **fertilizer**. Working with farm machinery can be very dangerous, too. Farm equipment causes about 12 percent of farm injuries in the U.S.

Tractors are the cause of many accidents on farms. Fitting them with roll bars and seat belts helps to reduce the number of injuries.

Areas where grain is stored, such as silos or barns, can be dangerous. People and animals can become trapped.

Organic Farming

Organic farming does not use any nonnatural pesticides. This type of farming may be better for the environment because the soil is not polluted, or made unsafe, with harmful chemicals. This keeps the soil healthy so it can be used to grow crops for many years in the future. Crops grown organically are believed to be healthier for people.

There are organic farms in all 50 states, but the state of California has the most, with more than 2,700.

The United States grows more organic apples than any other country. Farms in the state of Washington grow 80 percent of these apples, about

6 million boxes.

Foods that are labeled as organic have a seal from the United States Department of Agriculture.

Organic products are now sold in

73 percent

of all conventional grocery stores.

All in a Day's Work

A typical day as a farmhand starts early. On dairy farms, farmhands milk cows as early as 5 a.m. For farmhands working with livestock, feeding the animals and giving them fresh water is one of the first jobs of the day. They feed young or sick animals by hand or bottle. They must collect eggs from chickens before the eggs get too dirty or damaged. Farmhands move some types of livestock, such as cows, from their barns each day to graze in the fields. After caring for animals and cleaning stalls, a farmhand could repair machinery or buildings. Before the day is finished, farmhands check the animals once more. They round up the grazing livestock and bring them in for the night.

On farms that grow crops, harvesting must be done quickly. If crops are left too long, they may spoil, and the farmer will not be able to sell them.

Farmhands sometimes live on the farms where they work. This allows them to work whenever they are needed.

One bushel of wheat makes **210 servings** of spaghetti.

Kansas grows enough wheat each year to **feed every person in the world** for more than a week.

U.S. chickens produce almost **75 billion eggs** a year. This is enough for every person in the world to have about 10 eggs.

From the Farm to You

Farmers grow the foods people eat. Some crops, such as fruits and vegetables, are ready to eat as soon as they are harvested. Other foods, such as wheat and other grains, have to be processed before people can use them.

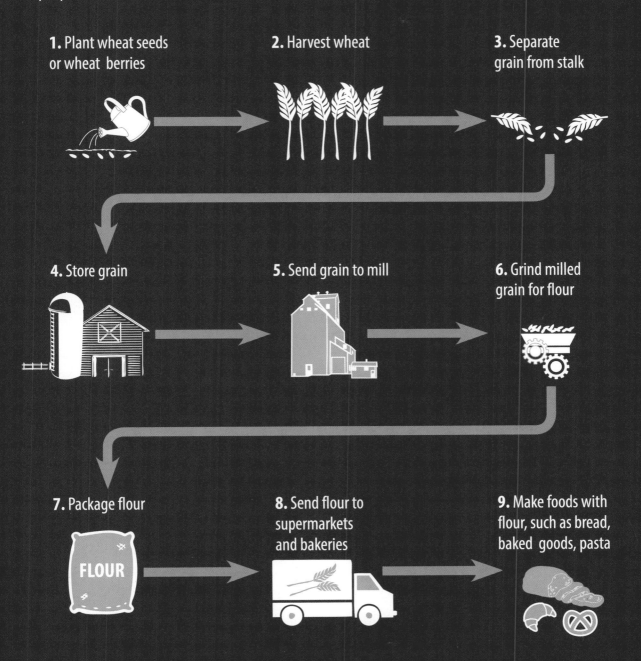

1. Plant wheat seeds or wheat berries

2. Harvest wheat

3. Separate grain from stalk

4. Store grain

5. Send grain to mill

6. Grind milled grain for flour

7. Package flour

8. Send flour to supermarkets and bakeries

9. Make foods with flour, such as bread, baked goods, pasta

FLOUR

Staying Safe

Farmhands are at risk of many dangers on a farm. They handle animals, operate machinery, and work with chemicals in their jobs. It is important that they take precautions for each type of job they are performing. Farmhands have to wear the proper safety equipment in order to stay safe on the job.

Mask or Respirator

Farmhands wear masks when spraying fertilizer or pesticide. The mask prevents the farmhand from breathing in chemicals that may be harmful. Masks can also be used in dusty conditions, such as working with grains and straw or harvesting crops.

Boots

Safety boots allow farmhands to work in dirty or wet conditions. The rubber keeps feet dry, and the special sole grips the slippery ground. A metal safety toe protects feet from heavy falling objects or animal hoofs.

Safety First

Each farm is responsible for providing a safe place to work. There are health and safety laws to protect agricultural workers. Farms must make sure machinery and equipment is safe and running properly. They must provide workers with bathrooms and water for drinking and hand-washing. Farms must also warn workers if they are working with hazards such as chemicals or sick animals.

Gloves

Farmhands use different types of gloves depending on the job they are doing. Thick leather gloves protect hands from cuts and scratches when doing rough work. Rubber-coated gloves provide a better grip for working with tools. Strong gloves made of nitrile rubber are the most puncture-resistant and are best for handling infectious material. They resist many chemicals and are most often used for wet jobs such as cleaning buckets or milking cows.

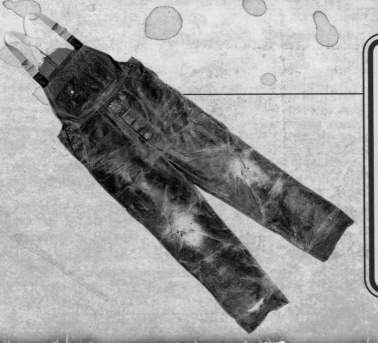

Coveralls

Coveralls, or overalls, are worn over the farmhand's regular clothing, protecting it from dirt and damage. After work, the dirty coveralls are taken off and may be used again the next day. Coveralls are made of a strong material like denim or canvas, and they come in many different colors.

Tools of the Trade

The most important tool in farming is the tractor. Tractors can be used for many types of jobs. Attaching different equipment can turn the tractor into a **plow** for breaking up soil, a seed drill or row planter for positioning seeds and planting them in rows, or a baler for making hay bales. Tractors can also be used to move heavy loads.

Types of Tractors

The most common types of tractors on a farm are utility, row crop, and compact tractors. Tractors are grouped by their size, weight, and the **horsepower** of their engines. Many farms have more than one type of tractor.

Utility Tractor
Utility tractors are tall and have powerful engines. They are used for many jobs on the farm, such as moving food, hay, or manure, hauling equipment, shoveling snow, or even digging holes for fence posts.

Row Crop Tractor

Row crop tractors are designed to work in fields without damaging the rows of growing plants. Another type of tractor, called the high crop tractor, can be used for very tall crops. These types of tractors can also perform many of the same jobs as utility tractors.

Compact Tractor

Smaller compact tractors are used on smaller farms or for specific jobs such as cleaning out animal stalls. They cannot be used for large or heavy jobs.

Then

Before the invention of the tractor in 1868, farmers worked their fields with horses and plows. One horse, or a team of horses, was hooked up to a plow made of wood and metal. The farmer or farmhand guided the horse and plow back and forth through the field.

Now

Tractors are used to pull plows today. Modern plows are made of steel. Some large plows can make up to 18 furrows, or grooves in the soil, at one time. A field that once took one and a half hours to plow with five horses takes as little as five minutes with one tractor today.

The Farmhand's Role

Farmhands work to help a farm run smoothly. Farming has a very important role in society—feeding people. Not everyone can farm in order to grow and raise food. Farmers and farmhands do this job for everyone, working to provide food and other products people can buy. On average, one farmer in the United States grows enough food to feed 144 people. Farms also provide jobs. More than 22 million people in the United States work in the agriculture industry.

"It's a dirty job, but someone has to do it."

Farming and the Environment

Farming land can be hard on the environment. Growing crops can cause a loss of soil, or erosion. It uses large amounts of water and energy as well. Farming can also leave less land for wildlife. Many farmers today use **sustainable** farming methods. This means they farm in a way that will keep the land and animals healthy for the future.

Crop rotation is one way farmers are taking care of the land. Growing different crops every year in the same field is healthier for the soil.

Exports

Exports are goods sold from one country to another. Different countries may have climates or land that is better suited to certain types of farms. They can export some of their farm products to other countries that want to buy them.

The state of California grows

80 percent

of the world's almonds.

Almost 25 percent of the products grown on U.S. farms are exported to other countries.

The U.S. exports about 65 percent of its cotton each year. That is more than 3 million bales of cotton, enough to make **600 million pairs of jeans**.

Every year, the U.S. exports enough beef to make nearly 10 billion quarter-pound burgers.

Becoming a Farmhand

To become a farmhand, people should enjoy physical work and working outside. This job often requires heavy lifting and long hours without a chance to sit down. Strength and physical fitness are important. Farmhands need good listening and problem-solving skills. They should be able to follow instructions and safely operate machinery. Most training is done on the job.

Salaries for farmhands vary depending on the type and size of the farm. Farmhands who work with crops may be paid slightly less than those who work on ranches or other farms with animals. The chart below shows the average annual salary for different positions in the farming and agriculture industry.

Average Salary per Year

Farmworkers, General Laborer	$20,040
Agricultural Graders and Sorters	$21,180
Farmworkers, Farm or Ranch	$24,040
Agricultural Equipment Operator	$25,970
Animal Breeder	$35,620
Agricultural Inspector	$42,340
Farm Supervisor	$45,040

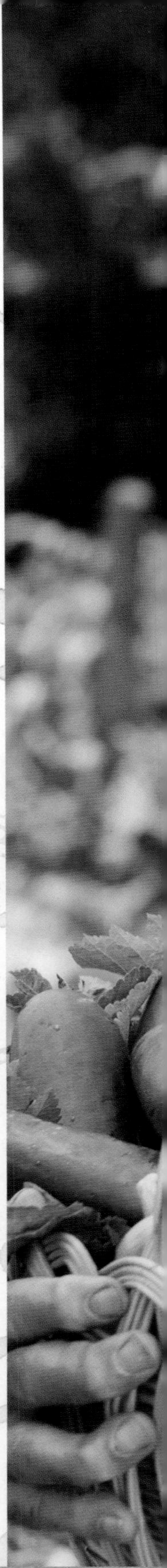

Farmhands need a wide variety of skills, most of which they learn by working on the farm.

Is This Career for You?

A career as a farmhand is not easy. The hours are long, and farmhands often work outside in bad weather. Working conditions on a farm can be dirty and smelly. However, working as a farmhand can be a rewarding and interesting job. Farmhands play an important role in providing food for people all over the world.

☑ ## Training
Farmhands are usually trained on the job by farmers or more experienced farmhands.

☑ ## Education
No special education is needed to be a farmhand. Courses on agriculture, animal handling, and operating farm machinery can be valuable if farming is a long-term career choice. A valid driver's license may be needed for driving tractors and wagons.

☑ ## Application
Apply for a job as a farmhand directly with the farm or through an agricultural employment company. Some jobs are seasonal.

Career Connections

Plan your career as a farmhand with this activity. Follow the instructions outlined in the steps to complete the process of becoming a farmhand.

 1. Speak to a farmer or farmhand. This person can answer your questions and give you an inside look at the position.

 2. Visit a job or agriculture trade fair to find out more information about working in the agriculture industry. Clubs like 4-H and National Future Farmers of America offer information and experience to children and young adults.

 **3.** Work on your resumé. A good resumé that shows your strongest skills can go a long way toward attracting the attention of potential employers.

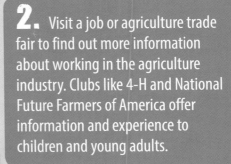 **4.** Call or write to a farm or agricultural business. Say that you are interested in a position as a farmhand and ask for advice on how to apply.

1. Decide if you have the personality and attitude to be a farmhand. If you do not mind a dirty job, can work flexible hours, and are in good physical shape, this may be the job for you.

2. Consider the skills you will need to have. Having knowledge about farming machinery and equipment will be a bonus.

3. Contact employers for requirements. Look for farms and agricultural companies. Get in touch with them and find out what they are looking for from potential applicants.

4. Apply for the position and arrange an interview. If successful, come to the interview with knowledge of the industry and your skills.

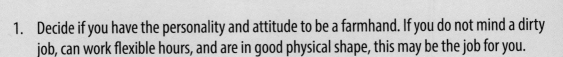

Quiz

1. What is another name for cleaning out animal stalls?

2. What do farmhands often wear over their clothing while they work?

3. What percentage of the U.S. population lives on farms?

4. What type of farming only uses natural pesticides?

5. What type of tractor is designed to work in fields without damaging the rows of growing plants?

6. How many servings of spaghetti does one bushel of wheat make?

7. What is another name for farm animals?

8. What percentage of products grown in the U.S. is exported to other countries?

9. When was the tractor invented?

10. How many people can one U.S. farmer's crops feed?

Answers: 1. mucking out
2. coveralls or overalls
3. 2 percent
4. organic farming
5. row crop tractor
6. 210 servings
7. livestock
8. 25 percent of all products
9. in 1868
10. 144 people

Key Words

fertilizer: a natural or chemical substance added to soil to help plants grow

graze: to feed on growing vegetation, such as grass

harvest: the season when crops are gathered

horsepower: a unit used to measure the power of engines

livestock: farm animals that are kept and raised for profit

manure: solid waste from farm animals; can be used as a natural fertilizer for growing plants

pesticides: chemicals used to kill animals or insects that are harmful to plants and crops

plow: farm equipment used to dig and turn over soil to prepare it for planting seeds

sustainable: methods that use, but do not destroy, land and natural resources

Index

Log on to www.av2books.com

AV² by Weigl brings you media enhanced books that support active learning. Go to www.av2books.com, and enter the special code found on page 2 of this book. You will gain access to enriched and enhanced content that supplements and complements this book. Content includes video, audio, weblinks, quizzes, a slide show, and activities.

AV² Online Navigation

Book Pages
AV² pages directly correspond to pages in the book.

Audio
Listen to sections of the book read aloud.

Video
Watch informative video clips.

Key Words
Study vocabulary, and complete a matching word activity.

Embedded Weblinks
Gain additional information for research.

Quizzes
Test your knowledge.

Slide Show
View images and captions, and prepare a presentation.

Try This!
Complete activities and hands-on experiments.

AV² was built to bridge the gap between print and digital. We encourage you to tell us what you like and what you want to see in the future.

Sign up to be an AV² Ambassador at www.av2books.com/ambassador.

Due to the dynamic nature of the Internet, some of the URLs and activities provided as part of AV² by Weigl may have changed or ceased to exist. AV² by Weigl accepts no responsibility for any such changes. All media enhanced books are regularly monitored to update addresses and sites in a timely manner. Contact AV² by Weigl at 1-866-649-3445 or av2books@weigl.com with any questions, comments, or feedback.